M000189706

# A
# *Scriptural*
# ROSARY

Compiled and with an Introduction by
Marianne Lorraine Trouvé, FSP

BOOKS & MEDIA
Boston

# INTRODUCTION

In his Apostolic Letter, *On the Most Holy Rosary,* Pope John Paul II invites us to "rediscover the Rosary in the light of Scripture." The Rosary is a way of contemplation, which simply means to look on the face of Christ. With Mary, we remember the mysteries of Jesus' life, and with her we "learn Christ." This "remembering" is "a making present of the works brought about by God in the history of salvation" (n. 13).

What a powerful statement! In this sense, to remember does not mean only to recall a past event. To prayerfully ponder God's saving works actually brings us under their saving influence. Praying the Scriptural Rosary is a way to do this because it brings us into contact with the word of God; it has power to change our lives. As the Pope put it: "We are certain that this is the word of God, spoken for today and spoken 'for me.' If received in this way, the word of God can become part of the Rosary's methodology of repetition without giving rise to the ennui derived from the simple recollection of something already well-known. It is not a matter of recalling information but of *allowing God to speak*" (*Rosarium,* n. 30).

God will say to us whatever we need to hear. Listening to that word in prayer—being attentive to the inspirations the Holy Spirit speaks in our hearts—can help us grow in holiness. Sometimes these inspirations come in the form of words from Scripture that we recall in various situations. Sometimes they are new ideas we suddenly grasp, like a flare lighting up the night sky. Praying the Rosary gives us the listening space we need in the midst of our busy lives. As the beads slip through our fingers, the repeated Hail Marys form a sort of "background music" that allows our hearts to absorb God's word. When this word takes root in our hearts and grows, our hearts expand and become open to receive grace more and more. "The word of God is living and effective, sharper than any two-edged sword, penetrating even between soul and spirit, joints and marrow, and able to discern reflections and thoughts of the heart" (Heb 4:12).

## *Some Practical Points*

This Scriptural Rosary book provides a verse from the Bible for each Hail Mary of the Rosary. The Scripture verses are meant to help you pray, so use them freely in whatever way you wish. You may choose to read each verse before each Hail Mary, or you may prefer to contemplate one thought for the entire decade or even the entire Rosary. Sometimes God speaks in a powerful way through one thought or even a single word. Stay with it for as long as you need to.

Although we can pray the various series of mysteries on any day, each sequence is generally prayed on certain days of the week as follows:

| | |
|---|---|
| Joyful | Monday and Saturday |
| Luminous | Thursday |
| Sorrowful | Tuesday and Friday |
| Glorious | Wednesday and Sunday |

## *The Prayers of the Rosary*

### The Apostles' Creed

I believe in God, the Father almighty, creator of heaven and earth. I believe in Jesus Christ, his only Son, our Lord. He was conceived by the power of the Holy Spirit and born of the Virgin Mary. He suffered under Pontius Pilate, was crucified, died and was buried. He descended to the dead. On the third day he arose again. He ascended into heaven, and is seated at the right hand of the Father. He will come again to judge the living and the dead. I believe in the Holy Spirit, the holy Catholic Church, the communion of saints, the forgiveness of sins, the resurrection of the body, and life everlasting. Amen.

**The Lord's Prayer**

Our Father, who art in heaven, hallowed be thy name; thy kingdom come; thy will be done on earth as it is in heaven. Give us this day our daily bread, and forgive us our trespasses, as we forgive those who trespass against us, and lead us not into temptation, but deliver us from evil. Amen.

**Hail Mary**

Hail Mary, full of grace! The Lord is with you. Blessed are you among women, and blessed is the fruit of your womb, Jesus. Holy Mary, Mother of God, pray for us sinners, now and at the hour of our death. Amen.

**Glory**

Glory to the Father, and to the Son, and to the Holy Spirit. As it was in the beginning, is now, and will be forever. Amen.

## Hail, Holy Queen

Hail, holy Queen, Mother of mercy, our life, our sweetness, and our hope! To you we cry, poor banished children of Eve; to you we send up our sighs, mourning and weeping in this valley of tears. Turn then, most gracious advocate, your eyes of mercy toward us, and after this our exile, show unto us the blessed fruit of your womb, Jesus. O clement, O loving, O sweet Virgin Mary.

For those unfamiliar with praying the Rosary, the following diagram may be of help.

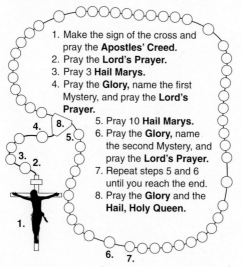

1. Make the sign of the cross and pray the **Apostles' Creed.**
2. Pray the **Lord's Prayer.**
3. Pray 3 **Hail Marys.**
4. Pray the **Glory,** name the first Mystery, and pray the **Lord's Prayer.**
5. Pray 10 **Hail Marys.**
6. Pray the **Glory,** name the second Mystery, and pray the **Lord's Prayer.**
7. Repeat steps 5 and 6 until you reach the end.
8. Pray the **Glory** and the **Hail, Holy Queen.**

# The
# Joyful Mysteries

# The First Joyful Mystery

## *The Annunciation*

∽

Mary's faith can also be compared to that of Abraham.... Abraham's faith constitutes the beginning of the Old Covenant; Mary's faith at the Annunciation inaugurates the New Covenant (*Mother of the Redeemer*, n. 14).

### *Our Father*

☞ God said to Abraham, "I will establish my covenant between me and you, and your offspring after you throughout their generations, for an everlasting covenant, to be God to you and to your offspring after you."

*Genesis 1:7*

### *Hail Mary*

☞ Those who believe are the descendants of Abraham.

*Galatians 3:7*

### *Hail Mary*

In the sixth month the angel Gabriel was sent by God to a town in Galilee called Nazareth, to a virgin engaged to a man whose name was Joseph, of the house of David. The virgin's name was Mary.

*Luke 1:26–27*

### Hail Mary

And he came to her and said, "Greetings, favored one! The Lord is with you."

*Luke 1:28*

### Hail Mary

But she was much perplexed by his words and pondered what sort of greeting this might be.

*Luke 1:29*

### Hail Mary

The angel said to her, "Do not be afraid, Mary, for you have found favor with God. And now, you will conceive in your womb and bear a son, and you will name him Jesus."

*Luke 1:30–31*

### Hail Mary

Mary said to the angel, "How can this be, since I am a virgin?"

*Luke 1:34*

### Hail Mary

☙ The angel said to her, "The Holy Spirit will come upon you, and the power of the Most High will overshadow you; therefore the child to be born will be holy; he will be called Son of God."

*Luke 1:35*

***Hail Mary***

☙ Then Mary said, "Here am I, the servant of the Lord; let it be with me according to your word." Then the angel departed from her.

*Luke 1:38*

***Hail Mary***

☙ But he [Jesus] said to them, "My mother and my brothers are those who hear the word of God and do it."

*Luke 8:21*

***Hail Mary***
***Glory be to the Father***

The Second Joyful Mystery

## *The Visitation*

❦

In the expression "Blessed is she who believed," we can therefore rightly find a kind of "key" which unlocks for us the innermost reality of Mary, whom the angel hailed as "full of grace" (*Mother of the Redeemer,* n. 19).

*Our Father*

↪ Now faith is the assurance of things hoped for, the conviction of things not seen.

*Hebrews 11:1*

*Hail Mary*

↪ Mary set out and went with haste to a Judean town in the hill country, where she entered the house of Zechariah and greeted Elizabeth.

*Luke 1:39–40*

*Hail Mary*

↪ When Elizabeth heard Mary's greeting, the child leaped in her womb. And Elizabeth was filled with the Holy Spirit.

*Luke 1:41*

*Hail Mary*

&#8766; [Elizabeth] exclaimed with a loud cry, "Blessed are you among women, and blessed is the fruit of your womb. And why has this happened to me, that the mother of my Lord comes to me?"

*Luke 1:42–43*

**Hail Mary**


&#8766; "For as soon as I heard the sound of your greeting, the child in my womb leaped for joy."

*Luke 1:44*

**Hail Mary**


&#8766; "And blessed is she who believed that there would be a fulfillment of what was spoken to her by the Lord."

*Luke 1:45*

**Hail Mary**


&#8766; "O daughter, you are blessed by the Most High God above all other women on earth; and blessed be the Lord God."

*Judith 13:18*

**Hail Mary**


&#8766; If you obey the LORD your God...blessed shall be the fruit of your womb.

*Deuteronomy 28:2, 4*

**Hail Mary**

ᔈ O the depth of the riches and wisdom and knowledge of God! How unsearchable are his judgments and how inscrutable his ways!

*Romans 11:33*

**Hail Mary**


ᔈ Mary said, "My soul magnifies the Lord, and my spirit rejoices in God my Savior, for he has looked with favor on the lowliness of his servant."

*Luke 1:46–48*

**Hail Mary**

**Glory be to the Father**

# The Third Joyful Mystery

## *The Birth of Jesus*

*Only when Christ is formed in us will the mystery of Christmas be fulfilled in us (CCC, n. 526).*

### *Our Father*

❧ And she gave birth to her firstborn son and wrapped him in bands of cloth, and laid him in a manger, because there was no place for them in the inn.

*Luke 2:7*

### *Hail Mary*

❧ [The shepherds] went with haste and found Mary and Joseph, and the child lying in the manger.

*Luke 2:16*

### *Hail Mary*

❧ But Mary treasured all these words and pondered them in her heart.

*Luke 2:19*

### *Hail Mary*

❧ God's love was revealed among us in this way: God sent his only Son into the world so that we might live through him.

*1 John 4:9*

**Hail Mary**

❧ In this is love, not that we loved God but that he loved us and sent his Son to be the atoning sacrifice for our sins.

*1 John 4:10*

**Hail Mary**

❧ For God so loved the world that he gave his only Son, so that everyone who believes in him may not perish but may have eternal life.

*John 3:16*

**Hail Mary**

❧ Indeed, God did not send the Son into the world to condemn the world, but in order that the world might be saved through him.

*John 3:17*

**Hail Mary**

❧ Long ago God spoke to our ancestors in many and various ways by the prophets, but in these last days he has spoken to us by a Son.

*Hebrews 1:1–2*

**Hail Mary**

In the beginning was the Word, and the Word was with God, and the Word was God.

*John 1:1*

*Hail Mary*

And the Word became flesh and lived among us, and we have seen his glory, the glory as of a father's only son, full of grace and truth.

*John 1:14*

*Hail Mary*

*Glory be to the Father*

# The Fourth Joyful Mystery

## *The Presentation in the Temple*

∽

Simeon's words seem like a second Annunciation to Mary, for they tell her of the actual historical situation in which the Son is to accomplish his mission, namely, in misunderstanding and sorrow (*Mother of the Redeemer,* n. 16).

### *Our Father*

✳ See, I am sending my messenger to prepare the way before me, and the Lord whom you seek will suddenly come to his temple.

*Malachi 3:1*

### *Hail Mary*

✳ When the time came for their purification according to the law of Moses, they brought him up to Jerusalem to present him to the Lord.

*Luke 2:22*

### *Hail Mary*

✳ Now there was a man in Jerusalem whose name was Simeon; this man was righteous and devout, looking forward to the consolation of Israel, and the Holy Spirit rested on him.

*Luke 2:25*

### *Hail Mary*

✳ Guided by the Spirit, Simeon came into the temple; and when the parents brought in the child Jesus...Simeon took him in his arms and praised God, saying...

*Luke 2:27–28*

### *Hail Mary*

✳ "Master, now you are dismissing your servant in peace, according to your word; for my eyes have seen your salvation..."

*Luke 2:29–30*

### *Hail Mary*

✳ "...which you have prepared in the presence of all peoples, a light for revelation to the Gentiles and for glory to your people Israel."

*Luke 2:31–32*

### *Hail Mary*

✳ Then Simeon blessed them and said to his mother Mary, "This child is destined for the falling and the rising of many in Israel, and to be a sign that will be opposed..."

*Luke 2:34*

### *Hail Mary*

✳ "...so that the inner thoughts of many will be revealed—and a sword will pierce your own soul too."

*Luke 2:35*

### *Hail Mary*

✳ There was also a prophet, Anna the daughter of Phanuel, of the tribe of Asher.... She never left the temple but worshiped there with fasting and prayer night and day.

*Luke 2:36–37*

**Hail Mary**

✳ At that moment she came, and began to praise God and to speak about the child to all who were looking for the redemption of Jerusalem.

*Luke 2:38*

**Hail Mary**

**Glory be to the Father**

## The Fifth Joyful Mystery

# *The Losing and Finding of Jesus in the Temple*

⌒

Contemplating the mystery of the hidden life of Jesus and the Blessed Virgin, we are invited to reflect on the mystery of our life which... "is hidden with Christ in God" (Col 3:3) (Pope John Paul II).

*Our Father*

❀ After three days they found him in the temple, sitting among the teachers, listening to them and asking them questions.

*Luke 2:46*

*Hail Mary*

❀ And all who heard him were amazed at his understanding and his answers.

*Luke 2:47*

*Hail Mary*

❀ His mother said to him, "Child, why have you treated us like this? Look, your father and I have been searching for you in great anxiety."

*Luke 2:48*

*Hail Mary*

❀ He said to them, "Why were you searching for me? Did you not know that I must be in my Father's house?"

*Luke 2:49*

### *Hail Mary*

❀ But they did not understand what he said to them.

*Luke 2:50*

### *Hail Mary*

❀ Then he went down with them and came to Nazareth, and was obedient to them. His mother treasured all these things in her heart.

*Luke 2:51*

### *Hail Mary*

❀ "The seed is the word of God.... But as for that in the good soil, these are the ones who, when they hear the word, hold it fast in an honest and good heart, and bear fruit with patient endurance."

*Luke 8:11, 15*

### *Hail Mary*

❀ "In my Father's house there are many dwelling places. If it were not so, would I have told you that I go to prepare a place for you?"

*John 14:2*

### *Hail Mary*

❀ "No one knows the Son except the Father, and no one knows the Father except the Son and anyone to whom the Son chooses to reveal him."

*Matthew 11:27*

**Hail Mary**


❀ Who is it that conquers the world but the one who believes that Jesus is the Son of God?

*1 John 5:5*

**Hail Mary**

**Glory be to the Father**

# THE LUMINOUS
# MYSTERIES

# The First Luminous Mystery

## *The Baptism of Jesus*

As Christ descends into the waters...the heavens open wide and the voice of the Father declares him the beloved Son (cf. Mt 3:17 and parallels), while the Spirit descends on him to invest him with the mission which he is to carry out (*Rosarium*, n. 21).

### *Our Father*

☞ God anointed Jesus of Nazareth with the Holy Spirit and with power.

*Acts 10:38*

### *Hail Mary*

☞ [John the Baptist] saw Jesus coming toward him and declared, "Here is the Lamb of God who takes away the sin of the world!"

*John 1:29*

### *Hail Mary*

☞ "I myself did not know him; but I came baptizing with water for this reason, that he might be revealed to Israel."

*John 1:31*

### *Hail Mary*

And John testified, "I saw the Spirit descending from heaven like a dove, and it remained on him."

*John 1:32*

### *Hail Mary*

"And I myself have seen and have testified that this is the Son of God."

*John 1:34*

### *Hail Mary*

In those days Jesus came from Nazareth of Galilee and was baptized by John in the Jordan.

*Mark 1:9*

### *Hail Mary*

And just as he was coming up out of the water, he saw the heavens torn apart and the Spirit descending like a dove on him.

*Mark 1:10*

### *Hail Mary*

And a voice came from heaven, "You are my Son, the Beloved; with you I am well pleased."

*Mark 1:11*

### *Hail Mary*

John said, "He who has the bride is the bridegroom. The friend of the bridegroom, who stands and hears him, rejoices greatly at the bridegroom's voice."

*John 3:29*

**Hail Mary**


"For this reason my joy has been fulfilled. He must increase, but I must decrease."

*John 3:30*

**Hail Mary**
**Glory be to the Father**

# *Jesus Reveals His Glory at the Wedding at Cana*

❧

Christ changes water into wine and opens the hearts of the disciples to faith, thanks to the intervention of Mary, the first among believers (*Rosarium*, n. 21).

### *Our Father*

❧ On the third day there was a wedding in Cana of Galilee, and the mother of Jesus was there.

*John 2:1*

### *Hail Mary*

❧ When the wine gave out, the mother of Jesus said to him, "They have no wine."

*John 2:3*

### *Hail Mary*

❧ And Jesus said to her, "Woman, what concern is that to you and to me? My hour has not yet come."

*John 2:4*

### *Hail Mary*

✣ His mother said to the servants, "Do whatever he tells you."

*John 2:5*

**Hail Mary**

✣ When the steward tasted the water that had become wine...the steward called the bridegroom.

*John 2:9*

**Hail Mary**

✣ He said to him, "Everyone serves the good wine first, and then the inferior wine after the guests have become drunk. But you have kept the good wine until now."

*John 2:10*

**Hail Mary**

✣ Jesus did this, the first of his signs, in Cana of Galilee, and revealed his glory; and his disciples believed in him.

*John 2:11*

**Hail Mary**

✣ The time is surely coming, says the LORD, when...the mountains shall drip sweet wine, and all the hills shall flow with it. I will restore the fortunes of my people Israel.

*Amos 9:13–14*

**Hail Mary**

☙ On this mountain the L ORD of hosts will make for all peoples a feast of rich food, a feast of well-aged wines...of well-aged wines strained clear.

*Isaiah 25:6*

### *Hail Mary*

☙ Thus says the L ORD: I remember the devotion of your youth, your love as a bride, how you followed me in the wilderness, in a land not sown.

*Jeremiah 2:2*

### *Hail Mary*
### *Glory be to the Father*

# The Third Luminous Mystery

## *Jesus Preaches the Kingdom and Calls Us to Conversion*

❧

Jesus proclaims the coming of the Kingdom of God, calls to conversion (cf. Mk 1:15), and forgives the sins of all who draw near to him in humble trust (cf. Mk 2:3–13; Lk 7:47–48) (*Rosarium*, n. 21).

### *Our Father*

❧ From that time Jesus began to proclaim, "Repent, for the kingdom of heaven has come near."

*Matthew 4:17*

### *Hail Mary*

❧ Jesus went throughout Galilee, teaching in their synagogues and proclaiming the good news of the kingdom and curing every disease and every sickness among the people.

*Matthew 4:23*

### *Hail Mary*

~ "The kingdom of heaven is like a mustard seed...; it is the smallest of all the seeds, but when it has grown it is the greatest of shrubs and becomes a tree."

*Matthew 13:31–32*

**Hail Mary**


~ "The kingdom of heaven is like yeast that a woman took and mixed in with three measures of flour until all of it was leavened."

*Matthew 13:33*

**Hail Mary**


~ "The kingdom of heaven may be compared to someone who sowed good seed in his field; but...an enemy came and sowed weeds among the wheat."

*Matthew 13:24–25*

**Hail Mary**


~ "The kingdom of heaven is like treasure hidden in a field, which someone found and hid; then in his joy he goes and sells all that he has and buys that field."

*Matthew 13:44*

**Hail Mary**


~ Lead a life worthy of God, who calls you into his own kingdom and glory.

*1 Thessalonians 2:12*

**Hail Mary**

Jesus answered, "Very truly, I tell you, no one can enter the kingdom of God without being born of water and Spirit."

*John 3:5*

### Hail Mary

Jesus said, "Let the little children come to me, and do not stop them; for it is to such as these that the kingdom of heaven belongs."

*Matthew 19:14*

### Hail Mary

For once you were darkness, but now in the Lord you are light. Live as children of light—for the fruit of the light is found in all that is good and right and true.

*Ephesians 5:8–9*

### Hail Mary
### Glory be to the Father

The Fourth Luminous Mystery

# *The Transfiguration*

～

The mystery of light *par excellence* is the Transfiguration.... The glory of the God-head shines forth from the face of Christ as the Father commands the astonished Apostles to "listen to him" (cf. Lk 9:35 and parallels) and to prepare to experience with him the agony of the Passion, so as to come with him to the joy of the Resurrection and a life transfigured by the Holy Spirit (*Rosarium*, n. 21).

### *Our Father*

✣ For it is the God who said, "Let light shine out of darkness," who has shone in our hearts to give the light of the knowledge of the glory of God in the face of Jesus Christ.

*2 Corinthians 4:6*

### *Hail Mary*


✣ Six days later, Jesus took with him Peter and James and John, and led them up a high mountain apart, by themselves.

*Mark 9:2*

### *Hail Mary*

✢ He was transfigured before them, and his clothes became dazzling white, such as no one on earth could bleach them.

*Mark 9:3*

### Hail Mary

✢ And there appeared to them Elijah with Moses, who were talking with Jesus.

*Mark 9:4*

### Hail Mary

✢ They appeared in glory and were speaking of his departure, which he was about to accomplish at Jerusalem.

*Luke 9:31*

### Hail Mary

✢ Then Peter said to Jesus, "Rabbi, it is good for us to be here; let us make three dwellings, one for you, one for Moses, and one for Elijah."

*Mark 9:5*

### Hail Mary

✢ Then a cloud overshadowed them, and from the cloud there came a voice, "This is my Son, the Beloved; listen to him!"

*Mark 9:7*

### Hail Mary

✢ Suddenly when they looked around, they saw no one with them any more, but only Jesus.

*Mark 9:8*

**Hail Mary**


✢ So we have the prophetic message more fully confirmed. You will do well to be attentive to this as to a lamp shining in a dark place, until the day dawns and the morning star rises in your hearts.

*2 Peter 1:19*

**Hail Mary**


✢ And all of us, with unveiled faces, seeing the glory of the Lord as though reflected in a mirror, are being transformed into the same image from one degree of glory to another; for this comes from the Lord, the Spirit.

*2 Corinthians 3:18*

**Hail Mary**

**Glory be to the Father**

The Fifth Luminous Mystery

## *Jesus Gives Us the Eucharist*

*Mary is a "woman of the Eucharist" in her whole life.* There is a profound analogy between the *Fiat* which Mary said in reply to the angel, and the *Amen* which every believer says when receiving the body of the Lord (*Ecclesia de Eucharistia* 53, 55).

**Our Father**

✾ Jesus knew that his hour had come to depart from this world and go to the Father. Having loved his own who were in the world, he loved them to the end.

*John 13:1*

**Hail Mary**

✾ The Lord Jesus on the night when he was betrayed took a loaf of bread, and when he had given thanks, he broke it and said, "This is my body that is for you."

*1 Corinthians 11:23–24*

**Hail Mary**

In the same way he took the cup also, after supper, saying, "This cup is the new covenant in my blood. Do this, as often as you drink it, in remembrance of me."

*1 Corinthians 11:25*

**Hail Mary**

For as often as you eat this bread and drink the cup, you proclaim the Lord's death until he comes.

*1 Corinthians 11:26*

**Hail Mary**

The cup of blessing that we bless, is it not a sharing in the blood of Christ? The bread that we break, is it not a sharing in the body of Christ?

*1 Corinthians 10:16*

**Hail Mary**

Because there is one bread, we who are many are one body, for we all partake of the one bread.

*1 Corinthians 10:17*

**Hail Mary**

Jesus said to them, "I am the bread of life. Whoever comes to me will never be hungry, and whoever believes in me will never be thirsty."

*John 6:35*

### *Hail Mary*

"Those who eat my flesh and drink my blood have eternal life, and I will raise them up on the last day."

*John 6:54*

### *Hail Mary*

You were ransomed from the futile ways inherited from your ancestors...with the precious blood of Christ, like that of a lamb without defect or blemish.

*1 Peter 1:18–19*

### *Hail Mary*

"Those who eat my flesh and drink my blood abide in me, and I in them."

*John 6:56*

### *Hail Mary*
### *Glory be to the Father*

# THE SORROWFUL
# MYSTERIES

The First Sorrowful Mystery

## *The Agony in the Garden*

∞

Although deeply troubled, Jesus does not flee before his "hour." ...He wanted his disciples to keep him company, yet he had to experience loneliness and abandonment (*Ecclesia de Eucharistia*, n. 4).

**Our Father**

❧ They went to a place called Gethsemane; and he said to his disciples, "Sit here while I pray."

*Mark 14:32*

**Hail Mary**

❧ And [he] said to them, "I am deeply grieved, even to death; remain here, and keep awake."

*Mark 14:34*

**Hail Mary**

❧ And going a little farther, he threw himself on the ground and prayed that, if it were possible, the hour might pass from him.

*Mark 14:35*

**Hail Mary**

He said, "Abba, Father, for you all things are possible; remove this cup from me; yet, not what I want, but what you want."

*Mark 14:36*

**Hail Mary**

In his anguish he prayed more earnestly, and his sweat became like great drops of blood falling down on the ground.

*Luke 22:44*

**Hail Mary**

Suddenly a crowd came, and the one called Judas, one of the twelve, was leading them. He approached Jesus to kiss him.

*Luke 22:47*

**Hail Mary**

But Jesus said to him, "Judas, is it with a kiss that you are betraying the Son of Man?"

*Luke 22:48*

**Hail Mary**

Then they seized him and led him away, bringing him into the high priest's house. But Peter was following at a distance.

*Luke 22:54*

**Hail Mary**

☙ Then Peter began to curse, and he swore an oath, "I do not know the man!" At that moment the cock crowed.

*Matthew 26:74*

**Hail Mary**

☙ The Lord turned and looked at Peter. Then Peter remembered the word of the Lord... "you will deny me three times." And he went out and wept bitterly.

*Luke 22:61, 62*

**Hail Mary**

**Glory be to the Father**

## The Second Sorrowful Mystery

# *The Scourging at the Pillar*

The mission of the only-begotten Son consists in *conquering sin and death*. He conquers sin by his obedience unto death, and he overcomes death by his resurrection (Pope John Paul II).

### *Our Father*

✤ Pilate said, "I have not found this man guilty of any of your charges against him."

*Luke 23:14*

### *Hail Mary*

✤ "Indeed, he has done nothing to deserve death. I will therefore have him flogged and release him."

*Luke 23:15–16*

### *Hail Mary*

✤ Then they all shouted out together, "Away with this fellow! Release Barabbas for us!"

*Luke 23:18*

### *Hail Mary*

❧ They kept urgently demanding with loud shouts that he should be crucified; and their voices prevailed.

*Luke 23:23*

### *Hail Mary*

❧ So Pilate...released the man they asked for, the one who had been put in prison for insurrection and murder, and he handed Jesus over as they wished.

*Luke 23:24–25*

### *Hail Mary*

❧ I gave my back to those who struck me, and my cheeks to those who pulled out the beard; I did not hide my face from insult and spitting.

*Isaiah 50:6*

### *Hail Mary*

❧ The righteous one, my servant, shall make many righteous, and he shall bear their iniquities.

*Isaiah 53:11*

### *Hail Mary*

❧ God proves his love for us in that while we still were sinners Christ died for us.

*Romans 5:8*

### *Hail Mary*

❧ But he was wounded for our transgressions, crushed for our iniquities.

*Isaiah 53:5*

*Hail Mary*

❧ Upon him was the punishment that made us whole, and by his bruises we are healed.

*Isaiah 53:5*

*Hail Mary*
*Glory be to the Father*

The Third Sorrowful Mystery

# *The Crowning with Thorns*

❧

Christ drew close above all to the world of human suffering through the fact of having taken *this suffering upon his very self* (Pope John Paul II).

**Our Father**

❧ Pilate asked Jesus, "Are you the King of the Jews?"

*John 18:33*

**Hail Mary**

❧ Jesus answered, "My kingdom is not from this world."

*John 18:36*

**Hail Mary**

❧ Then the soldiers of the governor took Jesus into the governor's headquarters, and they gathered the whole cohort around him.

*Matthew 27:27*

**Hail Mary**

❧ They stripped him and put a scarlet robe on him, and after twisting some thorns into a crown, they put it on his head.

*Matthew 27:28–29*

***Hail Mary***


❧ They put a reed in his right hand and knelt before him and mocked him, saying, "Hail, King of the Jews!"

*Matthew 27:29*

***Hail Mary***


❧ They spat on him, and took the reed and struck him on the head.

*Matthew 27:30*

***Hail Mary***


❧ They also blindfolded him and kept asking him, "Prophesy! Who is it that struck you?"

*Luke 22:64*

***Hail Mary***


❧ They kept heaping many other insults on him.

*Luke 22:65*

***Hail Mary***

❧ After mocking him, they stripped him of the robe and put his own clothes on him.

*Matthew 27:31*

**Hail Mary**

❧ "Jesus, remember me when you come into your kingdom."

*Luke 23:42*

**Hail Mary**

**Glory be to the Father**

The Fourth Sorrowful Mystery

## *The Carrying of the Cross*

In the cross of Christ not only is the redemption accomplished through suffering, but *also human suffering itself has been redeemed* (Pope John Paul II).

**Our Father**

✳ May I never boast of anything except the cross of our Lord Jesus Christ, by which the world has been crucified to me, and I to the world.

*Galatians 6:14*

**Hail Mary**

✳ So they took Jesus; and carrying the cross by himself, he went out to what is called The Place of the Skull, which in Hebrew is called Golgotha.

*John 19:16–17*

**Hail Mary**

✳ As they went out, they came upon a man from Cyrene named Simon; they compelled this man to carry his cross.

*Matthew 27:32*

**Hail Mary**

✳ A great number of the people followed him, and among them were women who were beating their breasts and wailing for him.

*Luke 23:27*

*Hail Mary*

✳ But Jesus turned to them and said, "Daughters of Jerusalem, do not weep for me, but weep for yourselves and for your children."

*Luke 23:28*

*Hail Mary*

✳ "Whoever does not carry the cross and follow me cannot be my disciple."

*Luke 14:27*

*Hail Mary*

✳ For the message about the cross is foolishness to those who are perishing, but to us who are being saved it is the power of God.

*1 Corinthians 1:18*

*Hail Mary*

✳ [Jesus] humbled himself and became obedient to the point of death—even death on a cross.

*Philippians 2:8*

*Hail Mary*

✳ For the sake of the joy that was set before him [Jesus] endured the cross, disregarding its shame.

*Hebrews 12:2*

**Hail Mary**

✳ For we do not have a high priest who is unable to sympathize with our weaknesses, but we have one who in every respect has been tested as we are, yet without sin.

*Hebrews 4:15*

**Hail Mary**

**Glory be to the Father**

# *The Crucifixion and Death of Jesus*

John at the foot of the cross somehow represents every man and woman for whom the motherhood of the Mother of God is spiritually extended (Pope John Paul II).

### *Our Father*

❀ And when they had crucified him, they divided his clothes among themselves by casting lots.

*Matthew 27:35*

### *Hail Mary*

❀ Then Jesus said, "Father, forgive them; for they do not know what they are doing."

*Luke 23:34*

### *Hail Mary*

❀ Meanwhile, standing near the cross of Jesus were his mother, and his mother's sister, Mary the wife of Clopas, and Mary Magdalene.

*John 19:25*

### *Hail Mary*

❧ When Jesus saw his mother and the disciple whom he loved standing beside her, he said to his mother, "Woman, here is your son."

*John 19:26*

**Hail Mary**

❧ Then he said to the disciple, "Here is your mother." And from that hour the disciple took her into his own home.

*John 19:27*

**Hail Mary**

❧ At three o'clock Jesus cried out with a loud voice, "Eloi, Eloi, lema sabachthani?" which means, "My God, my God, why have you forsaken me?"

*Mark 15:34, Psalm 22:1*

**Hail Mary**

❧ I am poured out like water, and all my bones are out of joint; my heart is like wax; it is melted within my breast.

*Psalm 22:14*

**Hail Mary**

❧ When Jesus knew that all was now finished, he said (in order to fulfill the Scripture), "I am thirsty."

*John 19:28*

**Hail Mary**

❀ A jar full of sour wine was standing there. So they put a sponge full of the wine on a branch of hyssop and held it to his mouth.

*John 19:29*

*Hail Mary*

❀ When Jesus had received the wine, he said, "It is finished." Then he bowed his head and gave up his spirit.

*John 19:30*

*Hail Mary*

***Glory be to the Father***

# THE GLORIOUS
# MYSTERIES

## *The Resurrection*

∽

By his death, Christ liberates us from sin; by his Resurrection, he opens for us the way to a new life (*CCC*, n. 654).

**Our Father**

🙪 "Do not be alarmed; you are looking for Jesus of Nazareth, who was crucified. He has been raised; he is not here."

*Mark 16:6*

**Hail Mary**

🙪 Now after he rose early on the first day of the week, he appeared first to Mary Magdalene.

*Mark 16:9*

**Hail Mary**

🙪 So if you have been raised with Christ, seek the things that are above, where Christ is, seated at the right hand of God.

*Colossians 3:1*

**Hail Mary**

☞ Clean out the old yeast so that you may be a new batch, as you really are unleavened. For our paschal lamb, Christ, has been sacrificed.

*1 Corinthians 5:7*

**Hail Mary**


☞ Therefore, let us celebrate the festival, not with the old yeast, the yeast of malice and evil, but with the unleavened bread of sincerity and truth.

*1 Corinthians 5:8*

**Hail Mary**


☞ We know that Christ, being raised from the dead, will never die again; death no longer has dominion over him.

*Romans 6:9*

**Hail Mary**


☞ So you also must consider yourselves dead to sin and alive to God in Christ Jesus.

*Romans 6:11*

**Hail Mary**


☞ Blessed be the God and Father of our Lord Jesus Christ! By his great mercy he has given us a new birth into a living hope through the resurrection of Jesus Christ from the dead.

*1 Peter 1:3*

**Hail Mary**

☙ If Christ has not been raised, then our proclamation has been in vain and your faith has been in vain.

*1 Corinthians 15:14*
***Hail Mary***


☙ "Where, O death, is your victory? Where, O death, is your sting?"

*1 Corinthians 15:55*
***Hail Mary***
***Glory be to the Father***

## The Second Glorious Mystery

### *The Ascension*

◌

Jesus Christ, the head of the Church, precedes us into the Father's glorious kingdom so that we, the members of his Body, may live in the hope of one day being with him for ever (*CCC,* n. 666).

#### *Our Father*

⊷ The eleven disciples went to Galilee, to the mountain to which Jesus had directed them.

*Matthew 28:16*

#### *Hail Mary*

⊷ Jesus told them, "Go therefore and make disciples of all nations, baptizing them in the name of the Father and of the Son and of the Holy Spirit."

*Matthew 28:19*

#### *Hail Mary*

⊷ "You will receive power when the Holy Spirit has come upon you; and you will be my witnesses in Jerusalem, in all Judea and Samaria, and to the ends of the earth."

*Acts 1:8*

#### *Hail Mary*

❧ When he had said this, as they were watching, he was lifted up, and a cloud took him out of their sight.

*Acts 1:9*

*Hail Mary*

❧ And if I go and prepare a place for you, I will come again and will take you to myself, so that where I am, there you may be also.

*John 14:3*

*Hail Mary*

❧ Each of us was given grace according to the measure of Christ's gift.

*Ephesians 4:7*

*Hail Mary*

❧ Therefore it is said, "When he ascended on high he made captivity itself a captive; he gave gifts to his people."

*Ephesians 4:8*

*Hail Mary*

❧ No one has ascended into heaven except the one who descended from heaven, the Son of Man.

*John 3:13*

*Hail Mary*

✐ Sing to God, sing praises to his name; lift up a song to him who rides upon the clouds.

*Psalm 68:4*

**Hail Mary**


✐ God has gone up with a shout, the Lord with the sound of a trumpet.

*Psalm 47:5*

**Hail Mary**

**Glory be to the Father**

The Third Glorious Mystery

# *The Descent of the Holy Spirit*

∾

Responding to the prayer of the Blessed Virgin and the community gathered in the upper room on the day of Pentecost, the Holy Spirit bestowed the fullness of his gifts on the Blessed Virgin and those present (Pope John Paul II).

### *Our Father*

∾ [The apostles] were constantly devoting themselves to prayer, together with certain women, including Mary the mother of Jesus, as well as his brothers.

*Acts 1:14*

### *Hail Mary*

∾ When the day of Pentecost had come, they were all together in one place.

*Acts 2:1*

### *Hail Mary*

∾ Suddenly from heaven there came a sound like the rush of a violent wind, and it filled the entire house where they were sitting.

*Acts 2:2*

### *Hail Mary*

✎ Divided tongues, as of fire, appeared among them, and a tongue rested on each of them.

*Acts 2:3*

### *Hail Mary*

✎ All of them were filled with the Holy Spirit and began to speak in other languages, as the Spirit gave them ability.

*Acts 2:4*

### *Hail Mary*

✎ In the last days it will be, God declares, that I will pour out my Spirit upon all flesh, and your sons and your daughters shall prophesy.

*Acts 2:17*

### *Hail Mary*

✎ "But the Advocate, the Holy Spirit, whom the Father will send in my name, will teach you everything, and remind you of all that I have said to you."

*John 14:26*

### *Hail Mary*

✎ He saved us, not because of any works of righteousness that we had done, but according to his mercy, through the water of rebirth and renewal by the Holy Spirit.

*Titus 3:5*

### *Hail Mary*

God's love has been poured into our hearts through the Holy Spirit that has been given to us.

*Romans 5:5*

**Hail Mary**


For all who are led by the Spirit of God are children of God.

*Romans 8:14*

**Hail Mary**

**Glory be to the Father**

# The Fourth Glorious Mystery

## *The Assumption*

❧

In her Assumption into heaven, Mary is as it were clothed by the whole reality of the communion of saints (*Mother of the Redeemer*, n. 41).

**Our Father**

✶ For as all die in Adam, so all will be made alive in Christ.

*1 Corinthians 15:22*

**Hail Mary**

✶ But each in his own order: Christ the first fruits, then at his coming those who belong to Christ.

*1 Corinthians 15:23*

**Hail Mary**

✶ [When] this mortal body puts on immortality, then the saying that is written will be fulfilled: "Death has been swallowed up in victory."

*1 Corinthians 15:54*

**Hail Mary**

✳ And those whom he predestined he also called; and those whom he called he also justified; and those whom he justified he also glorified.

*Romans 8:30*

### Hail Mary


✳ And this is the testimony: God gave us eternal life, and this life is in his Son.

*1 John 5:11*

### Hail Mary


✳ "O daughter, you are blessed by the Most High God above all other women on earth."

*Judith 13:18*

### Hail Mary


✳ Then God's temple in heaven was opened, and the ark of his covenant was seen within his temple.

*Revelation 11:19*

### Hail Mary


✳ A great portent appeared in heaven: a woman clothed with the sun, with the moon under her feet, and on her head a crown of twelve stars.

*Revelation 12:1*

### Hail Mary

✳ "And blessed is she who believed that there would be a fulfillment of what was spoken to her by the Lord."

*Luke 1:45*

*Hail Mary*

✳ "He has looked with favor on the lowliness of his servant...from now on all generations will call me blessed."

*Luke 1:48*

*Hail Mary*
*Glory be to the Father*

## *Mary Is Crowned Queen of Heaven and Earth*

∽

Mary, the handmaid of the Lord, has a share in this Kingdom of the Son. The *glory of serving* does not cease to be her royal exultation (*Mother of the Redeemer*, n. 41).

**Our Father**

❀ Jesus said, "You know that the rulers of the Gentiles lord it over them, and their great ones are tyrants over them."

*Matthew 20:25*

**Hail Mary**

❀ "It will not be so among you; but whoever wishes to be great among you must be your servant."

*Matthew 20:26*

**Hail Mary**

❀ "I confer on you, just as my Father has conferred on me, a kingdom, so that you may eat and drink at my table in my kingdom."

*Luke 22:29–30*

**Hail Mary**

❁ "For all who exalt themselves will be humbled, and those who humble themselves will be exalted."

*Luke 14:11*

**Hail Mary**


❁ "Be faithful until death, and I will give you the crown of life."

*Revelation 2:10*

**Hail Mary**


❁ Athletes exercise self-control in all things; they do it to receive a perishable wreath, but we an imperishable one.

*1 Corinthians 9:25*

**Hail Mary**


❁ She is more beautiful than the sun, and excels every constellation of the stars. Compared with the light she is found to be superior.

*Wisdom 7:29*

**Hail Mary**


❁ Who is this that looks forth like the dawn, fair as the moon, bright as the sun?

*Song of Songs 6:10*

**Hail Mary**

❁ I will greatly rejoice in the Lord, my whole being shall exult in my God; for he has clothed me with the garments of salvation.

*Isaiah 61:10*

**Hail Mary**

❁ He has covered me with the robe of righteousness, as a bridegroom decks himself with a garland, and as a bride adorns herself with her jewels.

*Isaiah 61:10*

**Hail Mary**

***Glory be to the Father***

**Pauline**
BOOKS & MEDIA

The Daughters of St. Paul operate book and media centers at the following addresses. Visit, call or write the one nearest you today, or find us on the World Wide Web, www.pauline.org

**CALIFORNIA**

| | |
|---|---|
| 3908 Sepulveda Blvd, Culver City, CA 90230 | 310-397-8676 |
| 5945 Balboa Avenue, San Diego, CA 92111 | 858-565-9181 |
| 46 Geary Street, San Francisco, CA 94108 | 415-781-5180 |

**FLORIDA**

| | |
|---|---|
| 145 S.W. 107th Avenue, Miami, FL 33174 | 305-559-6715 |

**HAWAII**

| | |
|---|---|
| 1143 Bishop Street, Honolulu, HI 96813 | 808-521-2731 |
| Neighbor Islands call: | 866-521-2731 |

**ILLINOIS**

| | |
|---|---|
| 172 North Michigan Avenue, Chicago, IL 60601 | 312-346-4228 |

**LOUISIANA**

| | |
|---|---|
| 4403 Veterans Memorial Blvd, Metairie, LA 70006 | 504-887-7631 |

**MASSACHUSETTS**

| | |
|---|---|
| 885 Providence Hwy, Dedham, MA 02026 | 781-326-5385 |

**MISSOURI**

| | |
|---|---|
| 9804 Watson Road, St. Louis, MO 63126 | 314-965-3512 |

**NEW JERSEY**

| | |
|---|---|
| 561 U.S. Route 1, Wick Plaza, Edison, NJ 08817 | 732-572-1200 |

**NEW YORK**

| | |
|---|---|
| 150 East 52nd Street, New York, NY 10022 | 212-754-1110 |
| 78 Fort Place, Staten Island, NY 10301 | 718-447-5071 |

**PENNSYLVANIA**

| | |
|---|---|
| 9171-A Roosevelt Blvd, Philadelphia, PA 19114 | 215-676-9494 |

**SOUTH CAROLINA**

| | |
|---|---|
| 243 King Street, Charleston, SC 29401 | 843-577-0175 |

**TENNESSEE**

| | |
|---|---|
| 4811 Poplar Avenue, Memphis, TN 38117 | 901-761-2987 |

**TEXAS**

| | |
|---|---|
| 114 Main Plaza, San Antonio, TX 78205 | 210-224-8101 |

**VIRGINIA**

| | |
|---|---|
| 1025 King Street, Alexandria, VA 22314 | 703-549-3806 |

**CANADA**

| | |
|---|---|
| 3022 Dufferin Street, Toronto, ON M6B 3T5 | 416-781-9131 |
| 1155 Yonge Street, Toronto, ON M4T 1W2 | 416-934-3440 |